A Time to Mourn, A Time to Dance

Life with our Children

By Evie McCandless

Desert Ministries, Inc.
Matthews, North Carolina

A TIME TO MOURN, A TIME TO DANCE

First Edition
©Copyright 2006 by
Desert Ministries, Inc.
P.O. Box 747
Matthews, North Carolina 28106-0747
ISBN 0-914733-33-8

Printed by Eagle Graphic Services, Fort Lauderdale, Florida

EDITOR'S COMMENTS

For a quarter of a century Desert Ministries Inc has reached out to those in "deserts" of human life, sharing the Living Water of Jesus Christ. In this present booklet, we offer a glimpse of how one family persevered in the Christian faith in spite of the great sadness in losing two of their three children. Dave and Evie McCandless have been dear friends to us for a long time. Peggy and I came into their lives at the time of Lynn's tragic death. I became close to their sons Mark and Jeff at that time. Even through God called me to a new ministry in Southeast Florida a long time ago, Peggy and I will always regard them as two of our dearest friends. My admiration of their faithfulness is unbounded. Their journey of faith is an inspiration. And, they are a joy to be with. God bless all of you who get to read this wonderful testimony. It will touch your life.

We will make it available to any and all who ask. If you would like to have additional copies, or if you desire a sample packet of some other books and booklets we publish, DMI will also make them available to you without charge. We survive and prosper by the blessings of God in the gifts of our friends and fellow travelers.

At present we have books: *When You Lose Someone You Love; Christ Will See You Trough; When Alzheimer's Strikes; A Journey Through Cancer; When Your Life Includes a Wheelchair; When a Child Dies;* and many more.

Write to Desert Ministries Inc. Box 747, Matthews NC, 28106. Call 704 849 0901. Or contact us on the web site: Desmin.org. Meanwhile, God bless you and keep you in His care.

Cordially,

Rev. Dr. Richard M. Cromie
President of Desert Ministries, Inc.

AUTHOR'S INTRODUCTION

We were surprised some time ago when Dr. Cromie asked us to write the story of how we have managed to cope with the death of two children who were taken away in their adult lives. It seemed an impossible assignment. Our friend Richard kept encouraging us, saying that our testimony would help endless numbers of people who also have to face the worst and still keep the faith.

We do not get through this mortal life without the love and care of many people. In our case, one of them is Richard Cromie. He and his wife Peggy spent many hours with us after Lynn was killed. He allowed us to vent our feelings and ask questions. He shared our hurt. He has been there for us so many times when we needed that special pastor and friend.

Another friend was helpful in editing the first draft and in helping to organize our thoughts. Still another helped us with the difficulties of the computer and typing. The dearest of close friends and relatives, who lived through our struggles, read and re-read the manuscript. They too, encouraged us by repeating that others would be helped by what we wrote. We are humbled to be asked to contribute to the work of Desert Ministries.

And, of course, we could not have dared to write without the guidance of God in the presence of the Holy Spirit. We pray that you the readers will be blessed and will find some new strength in Jesus Christ to guide and guard you on your way.

Dave and Evie McCandless

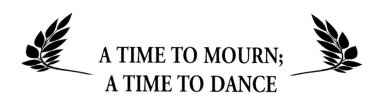

A TIME TO MOURN;
A TIME TO DANCE

Life with Our Children
By Evie McCandless

The phone at our bedside rang at 5:30 a.m. It was October 30, 2003. I heard a familiar voice say, "Mark is dead."

What? What are you saying?

"Mark went into the emergency room with blue alert and in three hours, he was gone."

How could that be? He was with us just one week ago. He was in perfect health. He and his brother competed on their water skis. Mark, our athlete, the masters swimmer. Mark, the son in hospital administration who was always to be here for us in our old age.

"He had been home feeling sick for two days; when he got to the hospital, he was in the last stages of bacterial meningitis. It takes you so very quickly."

Shock. Disbelief. Cry out to the Lord. Jesus, you have our daughter, why must you have Mark also?

I do not understand God's point of view here. I am no one special–why can't I have just an ordinary life with children and grandchildren? Our parents had it. My friends have it. I loved being a mom. I loved my children so very much. I know I could do a better job if I could do it over. But I can't. I am told to thank God in all circumstances. I have tried. It has been 30 years now since Lynn died. I have adjusted to this pretty well. There came a time when I believed that good came from her life and her death. Now that Mark is gone, I am crushed all over again. God must be very disappointed with me.

ave and I have been married 55 years. Most of the time, we have enjoyed good health. He likes to tell how we awake in the mornings. He says, "Are all systems go?" I say, "Yes, I think so." He says, "Are you deliriously happy?" I say, "Well, I'm happy."He likes to start my day with a chuckle or at least a smile.

As the children were growing up our favorite time of day was around the dinner table. We always ate at our round table, and Dave helped the children learn to visit and share their thoughts. He learned this from his family life with his parents and brothers. I like to think I influenced our children to love the outdoors. As a family, we hiked, camped, swam, and snow skied. I would like to be able to say we always went to church, but that came later. But we always said the blessing before our dinner.

We were a happy family. We enjoyed sports together. We celebrated all birthdays and holidays in a special way. We had dogs, friends, activities, big and little toys. What can I say?–we were privileged. I think we knew it, but we did take it all for granted. If it suited us to go camping, or skiing, or to our cottage for a weekend, we were off. That meant that church attendance was also taken for granted.

We participated when it was convenient. We sent our children to church camp in the summer. One summer I know our daughter Lynn received Jesus as her savior.

We have one more child, Jeff, our youngest. Jeff lives near enough that he came to cry with us. Then Debbie came after sending the children off to school. Next, our pastor and many dear friends arrived. We held hands and prayed. Of course, there were many phone calls to be made to relatives and friends, and arrangements had to be made to fly to where Mark lived. Looking back, it's easy to see the Lord holding us up. Precious friends took our dog, saw us off at the airport. When we arrived at Mark's home, the neighbors were there with a table full of their special dishes, and their hugs and warm welcome.

The day was Dave's birthday. Mark's birthday card came to his Dad the day he died along with his thoughtful gift certificate. The day also was All Saints Day, October 31. My entry in my diary that day is "Mark is in Heaven."

At Mark's funeral, the priest asked me if I would care to read scripture. The Lord lifted me up and I was in the pulpit before I had time to think otherwise. I had thought about it the night before, so I knew I wanted to read Isaiah 55: 12, 13, 8, 9. (I have written in my Bible, "this is a promise")

> *For you shall go out in joy, and be led forth in peace;*
> *The mountains and the hills before you shall break forth*
> *into singing,*

And all the trees in the field shall clap their hands.

*For my thoughts are not your thoughts, neither are your
    ways my ways,
Says the Lord.
For as the heavens are higher than the earth,
So are my ways higher than your ways
And my thoughts than your thoughts.*

There were many beautiful testimonies at the funeral.
Mark's special friend Andy had made all the arrangements.
He was brave and strong. He knows the Lord, and his sup-
port group was there. Half the hospital staff where Mark
worked was there and the other half of the sanctuary was
filled with the swimming team. Not all were believers. We
believe some are now seekers.

Both Dave and Jeff spoke standing beside the casket.
We took Mark's ashes to Pittsburgh where our children
grew up and placed them in the Columbarium beside his
sister Lynn. We were warmly received in Pittsburgh by so
many dear friends and relatives. And we were blessed with
a loving service to remember Mark. A precious friend of
Lynn's sang "On Eagles Wings," "The Lord's Prayer," and
"My Tribute." "To God be the glory for the things He has
done. With His blood, He has saved me. With His power, He
has raised me. To God be the glory for the things He
has done."

We went through Mark's things and brought home a few to hold and keep close. Life must go on. Now I must live for those near me. Relationships took on new meaning. We were overwhelmed at times by the acts of kindness we received. Cards, flowers, letters, food, books, phone calls, poems, plants, and especially prayers. I have loved the promises in the Bible, and they all take on deeper meanings for me now. God must know how much I need Him.

The big hurdle after the death of the loved one is getting through special days – holidays, birthdays, vacations. We find we must do them differently. We can't repeat the old ways – they will never be the same. We must keep their name present in our conversations. Find people who will let you do that. Not everyone will.

I am putting together a memory book about Mark. He was 49 years old, so we had a lot of years of sharing thoughts, places, people, and events. I remember, after Lynn died, my worst fear was that I would forget things about her. Of course, I never have. But at that time I would write down everything that came to my memory about her. I have not had to reread it. Thank you, Jesus.

Dave is tearing the front brick walk apart. He has put in a new fountain/bird bath and the cord needs to be buried. This reminds me of the day after Lynn's funeral. Dave went to the basement and began tearing out a cement wall. He took his anger out on that wall. But he had a goal. His workshop was much too big and my laundry room was quite small. My new room was finished with carpeting, a long counter top, new lighting; a very pleasant work room.

I need a way to vent my anger.

LYNN ANN

Lynn Ann was born on Labor Day, September 1, 1952. We gave her part of my name (Evalyn Ann). She had blue eyes and blond hair. The rest of our family were brown-eyed with dark hair. Her daddy soon called her "princess." Later in her life when she amazed me at what she could accomplish, I would wonder, whose child is she? She doesn't take after me. Now I know she was always God's child, lent to us for a few wonderful years.

We mothers in those days were kept in the hospital for a full week. My mother came to help me when we took our beautiful, perfect child home. I had to do everything by the book. My mother had raised four very healthy children, but we had to bathe the baby as the book described: hold the baby securely with left hand, as you gently sponge the little body. One day I called my pediatrician to ask why Lynn was crying. He said "there are a dozen reasons why newborns cry." I said, "OK, I have my pencil, I am ready. Tell me the twelve reasons." Well, it got better, and she was a very happy child. I felt I was receiving a report card on mothering when Lynn brought home her first report card from kindergarten. The teacher told how she knew Lynn came from a very happy home and was well loved. Thank you Jesus for that sweet memory.

Lynn was a little ballerina, she loved her Brownie troop, and always wanted to please her teachers and her parents. She was a good student. In eighth grade she was given the American Legion distinguished student award. This made us very proud. A happy time of day was when she practiced her piano lessons while I was in the kitchen preparing dinner. While our sons were becoming active in swimming meets, Lynn enjoyed working out with her synchronized swimming team. She had a great group of friends in high school. She was a cheerleader. I can see her in front of the sliding glass door where she could see her reflection, practicing the new routines. This made attending school activities fun watching her and her friends.

We sent our children to a summer Christian camp. Lynn went for five summers and then became a counselor the last two summers. She was active in Young Life. Many meetings were held in our home with a hundred kids packed in. A couple of seasons, the meetings were held in our church, and we participated by helping in the kitchen with the pancake breakfasts. They started at 7 a.m. They ate, heard a Christian message, and walked on to school. Those were good days.

Lynn chose Purdue University for her college years. Here she became active in the Navigator organization. She joined a sorority and led a Bible study in the House. In fact, after her death, the sorority established a memorial in her honor. Each year one girl was chosen to receive The Lynn McCandless Award given to the girl who exemplified Christian qualities within the House. We were always pleased to learn of this annual event, and we sent a gold cross to her. I loved writing the recipient a letter telling her how we were also honored to be part of the celebration.

During these years, we had a cottage on a lake. We spent many weekends there with family and friends. Lynn loved riding the motorcycle over the country roads. She was a willing crew for the sailing races. And water skiing–everyone loved that! In fact, the last picture I took of Lynn she had just let go of the rope and was gliding. I know of one heart she had broken in college. She felt the young man wasn't interested in knowing Jesus as his savior.

God had a purpose for Lynn's life and she was obedient. She had a poster in her room which read "I'm third. God first, others second and myself third." Lynn's life affected my life in many ways. She made me a better person. I will never forget her standing in the kitchen doorway before she left for school. I had complained that she had not made her bed, etc., etc. She said, "Mom, you never mention anything on all the days that I do make my bed." You know, I thought about that. I began to see myself as I was and I didn't like it. Then the big event was on a

Mother's weekend at college. She sat me down in her dorm room and said, "Mother, I want to take you through the four spiritual laws." I did not know what she was talking about, but I thought if this is what she wants to do, it's OK with me. So, she told me God loves me and wants me to have eternal life (John 3:16). Our sin separates us from God (Isaiah 59:2). God sent Jesus to restore our relationship with Him (John 5:24). And our response is to receive Jesus as our Savior (John 1:12) She was so sincere. I had realized that she loved the Lord, read her Bible a lot, and was a happy kid. So I prayed the sinners prayer with her. "Dear Lord Jesus, I know that I am sinful and need Your forgiveness. I believe that You died to pay the penalty for my sin. I want to turn from my sin and follow You instead. I invite You to come into my heart and life. In Jesus' name, I pray. Amen."

Nothing happened to me then, but back home, I suddenly found a neighborhood Bible study that many of my friends were in. I started going to a weekly prayer meeting. I began growing in the knowledge of God. Lynn and I had such fellowship together with my newfound faith. In retrospect, I see God was preparing me for what was to come. Lynn taught me that God has a plan for each life. We had three years of sharing Christ. Bless her heart. She didn't stop there. Another very memorable occasion was when Lynn sat Mark down at the kitchen table and took him through the four spiritual laws. I was in the family room sitting in the rocking chair, and watching TV. Lynn came to me and said "We have a new babe in Christ." I went into the kitchen and saw Mark looking like an angel. I could almost see a halo around his head. He was probably 15. He had just received Jesus as his Savior. How I cherish that memory.

Lynn also had the quality of changing a tense situation into a humorous one. She would mimic you and make you see how funny the problem really was, and we would all laugh. I miss that as much as anything. We also began to see how so much of life was following the crowd instead of doing your own thing. Her last three Christmases, we changed our routine. A couple of days before, we packed a few things, and went to our cottage to celebrate Christ's birth our way. We agreed we only needed one or two gifts each. We bought the last small live tree at the last gas station, and trimmed it with popcorn and cranberries on thread. We built a big fire in the stone fireplace. Of course, we brought the turkey and all the trimmings. On Christmas Eve, Lynn led us in our devotional. We had candles, we all sang, read about the birth of Christ, and prayed together. On Christmas Day we opened our gifts and ate dinner, played outside in the snow, and were just together. Back home were the parties and the busy work we decided we did not need. I will mention here that the Christmas after Lynn died, Mark took her place and led us in the Christmas devotional. The cottage became a place of retreat for me. The thing I needed most was to be with my family.

I do need to tell you what happened. It was Lynn's last year of college. She had a summer job. She was studying to be a dietician and had been hired by Allegheny General Hospital in her chosen field. She loved the work and the people. We gave her a yellow VW bug to get to and from. Mark also had a summer job working as a painter. They made arrangements to meet after work and drive together to our cottage. It was the Fourth of July holiday. We had already gone to the cottage to get ready for everyone. Their car was hit broadside by a drunk driver at an intersection where they had the right of way. Mark told us later that they had been telling each other stories of their day and were laughing. Mark had on his seat belt. Lynn did not. She was such a free spirit. Lynn hit the windshield and I know went immediately into the arms of Jesus. She was dead on arrival at the nearest university hospital. Mark was taken to the local hospital. We got a phone call—I sure don't know from whom. We gathered up Jeff, informed Dave's brother, and left in a hurry in a car I know had no gasoline, and drove over roads we didn't know in the pitch dark. A nurse met us and gave me a ring and a cross Lynn had been wearing. Later Dave's brother went to the scene of the accident and found Lynn's Bible in perfect condition. Everything else was towed away. We found Mark who was patched up and told him we had lost his sister. He had continually repeated our cottage phone number. This was July 3, 1973. Lynn was 20 years old.

The assistant pastor sat at our kitchen table for three days as friends and family came with comfort food. I can't tell you what he did or said. He was just there for us. I told him that I had bought a new dress for the service. "If this were Lynn's wedding, I would buy a new dress." Lynn's funeral was a celebration. She had graduated. Friends who played their guitars led the singing. "Pass It On," "They'll know we are Christians by our love, by our love, they'll know we are Christians by our love," and Bill Gaither's "Jesus, Jesus, Jesus, there's just something about that name. Jesus, Jesus, Jesus, like the fragrance after the rain. Jesus, Jesus, Jesus, let all heavens and earth proclaim, Kings and kingdoms will all pass away, there's just something about that name." Our senior pastor returned from his vacation to be with us. Lynn's sorority sisters traveled many miles to be with us. Mark was with us with his leg in a cast. Jeff and our German Shepard were always near. Do you see the thread running through this? "Be with us." That is all one can do for a bleeding heart–just BE there.

I kept reminding myself of Lynn's faith and that I could not let her down. After all she taught me that God had a plan for each life. This was God's plan for Lynn. In time I would see the answers to why. Each morning during the year following her death, I took her Bible and sat with it on my lap in the living room. I would turn pages and look for underscored verses and her comments in the margin. There were her messages to me. Then there were the days when I could not stop crying. Friends sat with me. I cleaned the oven better than it had ever been cleaned, mostly with tears. One friend came in crying so hard, and I said "what is it?" She said she was crying for me. Then I read in my Bible Romans 12:15, "Rejoice with those who rejoice; weep with those who weep." That is friendship.

There was the day I came across Matthew 10:37,38. "He who loves father or mother more than me is not worthy of me; and he who loves son or daughter more than me is not worthy of me; and he who does not take his cross and follow me is not worthy of me." That stopped me cold. That was me— I was loving Lynn more than everything and certainly more than I loved God. That verse really spoke to my heart. It took me a while to digest this revelation, but I did. I confessed my need for God to be first, and I let go of Lynn. You know that is when healing begins. We must let go.

For Christmas, 1971, Lynn inscribed a book to me. "Dear Mom, I am so thankful and proud to have a mother like you! There are very few daughters who are lucky enough to be able to share everything with their mothers.

And that only comes by having Christ at the center of our relationship. I pray that by this book you will realize more of Christ's love for us, His faithfulness, joy and peace." The book is COME AWAY MY BELOVED by Frances J. Roberts. Her words and the book continue to be a blessing to me. I long to hold her again, to laugh and to hear her sweet voice.

HERE IS HOW GOD WORKS

You know Romans 8:28. "All things work together for good for those who love God and are called according to His purpose." I went to a Womens Association meeting and heard the guest speaker, the director of Youth Guidance, Pittsburgh. He explained that the purpose of their organization was to reach out to troubled children in the inner city. They trained volunteers, place them with a child, and were the home base for further guidance. I felt a nudge to pursue this. The training was to secure you in your faith, and to match you with a child. The commitment was to take the Christian preparation course, promise to see your young person once a week and be faithful to see her for the next year. The child they matched me with was not a troubled youth, but she came from a dysfunctional family and her older sister had a volunteer. They thought it would be nice for Clare to have a volunteer also. Clare was an active eleven year old with blond hair, and very intelligent. When I learned her birthday was July 3rd (the date of Lynn's death) and she could do cartwheels wherever we went, I knew this was from God. Lynn always did cartwheels. Clare and I saw more of Pittsburgh than I had ever known. We exposed her to the suburbs, our lake cottage, and a bigger world. Her sister's volunteer was a lovely young woman and we often did things together. This also filled a need in my life. Our friendship with Clare continued through the following years. We were delighted to be guests at her wedding. Today Clare and her husband are living in a residential community with a good school system for their two sons. We keep in touch a couple of times a year. Her sons are being raised in a Christian home, and she loves the Lord. I have been so blessed by this friendship. Also, the Youth Guidance people were a great blessing.

I began to see that life is God's school for us. Each test makes us grow and change. We needed to be in a Christ-centered church and in fellowship with believers. We found this in a small Bible Chapel. We both began to listen more closely to the Word of God, and we were baptized by immersion. Our testimony was from Romans 10:9– "Confess with your lips that Jesus is Lord and believe in your heart that God raised Him from the dead, and you will be saved."

Healing is a long process. Shortly after Lynn died, we were invited to attend a weekend with the Pittsburgh Experiment. They held a weekend conference at Ogleby State Park. Just being away with loving friends, surrounded by God's beautiful country, and hearing Christian messages was a welcome retreat. Part of the experiment was to sit in small groups and deal with a personal issue. We called it "knee to knee" confession. I must say I cried a lot. But when one lady told me I had given her courage to go home to her own problem, I couldn't believe my ears. What that did for me was a surprise. I had helped someone else. That amazed me. As time passed, I realized how much her remark helped me in my healing. A friend gave me this scripture and I claimed it as a promise from God for me. 1 Peter 5:10 says "And after you have suffered a little while, the God of all grace, who has called you to His eternal glory in Christ, will Himself restore, establish, and strengthen you." These promises keep me encouraged.

MARK

Mark was a very special child. He seemed especially close to me. He was quiet and thoughtful. He was shy around strangers. He was very helpful to me in keeping watch over his little brother. Jeff was four years younger and a very active little guy. I could depend on Mark to do whatever was needed. I remember Mark's first day of school and how Jeff and I missed him.

That was a long day without Mark.

Through Mark's school years, he seemed to bloom more each year. He started out reticent and timid. In high school, he came into his own and his sister was so proud when she would hear his name announced on the speaker, along with the other athletes who performed well that day. Mark loved his swimming and he earned many medals in high school and in college at Penn State. Mark finished his education at the University of Pittsburgh with a masters degree in hospital administration.

Mark began his professional career in Philadelphia and continued there until be became Vice President of his hospital. At the time of his death, he was being considered for the position of President.

When Mark was a student, he was home for a weekend and brought one of his college friends. I was in Mark's room putting away some things, when I came across a book that had to do with homosexuality. After dinner and they had gone out, I talked with Dave about it. Mark returned home and Dave called him into our bedroom. They sat in the den just off our room. I sat on the edge of the bed. I was there but also separate from them. Dave was very gentle and asked Mark if he would like to tell us about the book. Mark was very frightened but he was able to tell his dad that he believed he was gay. He was not in a relationship, but believed that he needed to come to terms with it. All I can tell you about this is that God so filled me with love for that boy that all we could do was cry, and let him know we were there for him, and that we loved him very much. I am pleased to say we have always felt that way. That kind of love can only come from God. We hated the fact that our son was homosexual. He did not like it either. His statement to me was, "Mother, do you think I would choose this? This is not an easy way of life. It is very difficult." He honestly believed that he did not choose to be gay; that he was made that way and that he would find a way to live with it.

We went through many stages. Grief. My precious son would never have a wife and children. I always said he would make the best husband and father. Anger. It hurts so much when you hear jokes and expressions that belittle gay people. No compassion. We could not talk about this problem. When Lynn died, we were surrounded with loving and caring friends. We could not talk about this. We couldn't cry and share our hurt. We had to live the secret in privacy. We were totally humbled. We sought ministries that dealt with this and that probably proved to educate us, but didn't change Mark.

Mark came home often and brought his friends. We were all able to sit and talk and share our beliefs, our faith in God, our feelings. These young men are very intelligent, successful, compassionate, athletic and religious. We went through hard times learning to accept this fact about Mark but love always prevailed and for that I am so very thankful. We know of families that have estranged themselves from each other. I could never live with that. We needed Mark to continue to be a firm part of our family. And Mark needed us. When Jeff got married, Mark was his best man. When Jeff had his family, Mark was the devoted uncle. When Mark returned to his first love, swimming, and became a Masters swimmer, we were there to cheer for him.

JEFF

As a little boy, Jeff was a champion at composing his own prayers. One time on a camping trip, we were all in the car but Jeff, and almost drove off when a knock on the door alerted us to Jeff on the outside. I opened the door, and he said, "You wouldn't forget precious little me." His nick name after that was "Precious."

Jeff wasn't always precious. As a teenager he gave us many anxious moments. He wrecked a few cars, almost drowned in the middle of a frozen lake, had parties at our house when we were out of town, and Mark had to straighten it out with the police, to name just a few.

Mark was the dependable big brother to Jeff from the time he was four. In their adult years, Mark and Jeff took their annual ski trip together, a different place every year, and Mark made all the plans. All Jeff had to do was show up.

Lynn had been active in the Navigator organization while a student at Purdue. A few months after her death, the leaders of the Navigators visited us in Pittsburgh. This lovely couple and their two young children were gathered with us around our dining room table. The doorbell rang.

Dave answered the door and found a stranger there asking for the plants he came to get from our son Jeff. What plants, we wondered, and remembered the beautiful "tomato" plants he had been nursing in the window box of his bedroom. We'd remarked on how much attention he had paid to them. Dave and Jeff went upstairs and Jeff confessed to his dad that they were indeed marijuana plants. The plants were quickly disposed of and the man at the door was asked to leave. During this time, I was going from the dining room to the door and back, keeping all this from the respected guests in our home.

Jeff would not take his school work seriously. During his early years, I would often get called in for teacher conferences. He was in third grade and had been throwing spit balls (one hit a teacher). This time there were three women teachers and one man and myself sitting in a circle. I got all their complaints about him. In desperation, I exclaimed, "when you see him coming through the door of your room, stop for a moment and say a prayer for him." The male teacher said thoughtfully, "That's a good idea." Little did I know then as I know now. In Jeremiah 29, God tells us "I know the plans I have for you, for your welfare and not for evil, to give you a future and a hope. Then you will call upon me and come and pray to me, and I will hear you. You will seek me and find me; when you seek me with all your heart, I will be found by you."

Jeff has come close to death many times that we know of. There are probably more times we don't know about, and that is a blessing. One March when the waters of Deep Creek Lake are still freezing cold, Jeff and some friends skipped school and went to our cottage. Three boys took the fishing boat out to the middle and before long they found themselves in the water with a turned-over boat. That time of year there is no one on the lake and no one in the cabins, as this is a weekend resort. The boys became exhausted and terrified. Jeff decided the only chance of survival was for him to swim to shore. It wasn't long before he realized he wasn't going to succeed, and he was thinking, "I am drowning." God was at work. There were two men working the coves checking on the fishing conditions to report to the State as to the need for stocking the lake for fishing. They were cold and said to each other, "let's quit early." One man said, "after we check one more cove, we'll go in." It was then that they saw Jeff–probably getting his last breath. They pulled him out and he was able to tell them about his friends. They were all rescued. This incident was reported in the local newspaper so I learned the names of the men God sent to save Jeff, and I wrote to them to thank them. One called me and said he really felt it was a miracle that the boys survived those cold waters. And a miracle that they hadn't turned in early as it was very foggy and they were freezing. A few days after this, I was reading Isaiah 43. I put Jeff's name and the date beside this scripture. "Fear not for I have redeemed you; I have called you by name, you are mine. When you pass through the waters I will be with you. For I am the Lord your God." That was a time to praise the Lord.

The major life saving event for Jeff was with his airplane. He calls it his "falling off the mountain." He and a buddy flew to the highest mountain in North Carolina to a resort with a landing strip–they called it an air port. It was not equipped with a tower or radio or attendant. They had a girl selling candy. Well, Jeff had trouble landing and broke the landing gear. But they fulfilled their mission and played golf. They slept fitfully worrying about the trip home. The plane could not get enough speed to take off so at the end of the one landing strip, the plane nose-dived over the cliff. It came to a stop upside down with the cockpit in a ditch. The boys, hanging in their seat belts, managed to get free and out of the plane. They knew it could go up in flames, but it did not. The accident was seen, so an ambulance was soon there. They were taken to the emergency trauma unit of a Charlotte Hospital. His friend was not hurt and he stayed with Jeff. Jeff had a broken back. We were summoned and his family was soon around him. A steel rod was put along his spine. When he complained of his pain, the doctor said, "you are lucky to be alive."

While flat on his back in the hospital, a business acquaintance called him. He said, "Jeff, if you were to die today, do you know where you will go?" Jeff said, "no." The man asked, "do you want to know God and be assured of your salvation?" Jeff said, "yes." There was a Bible near him and this man God sent to Jeff led him through the scriptures and to John 3:16 "For God so loved the world that he gave His only Son, that whoever believes in Him should not perish but have eternal life." Jeff received Jesus into his heart and was born again. After he returned to Hilton Head, he and Debbie found this man of God, and they were baptized. We really praised our Lord. This was a time to shout for joy. He not only saved his physical life, He also saved his eternal life. That is an AMEN.

Jeff is now the owner of his very successful business. He is in good health and is very active. He and Debbie have our three beautiful grandchildren. We are privileged to live near enough that we can see each other as much as we like. We worship together in church on Sundays; always spend birthdays and holidays together.

Ecclesiastes tells us there is a time for everything. "For everything there is a season, and a time for every matter under heaven. A time to be born, a time to die. A time to weep, and a time to laugh. A time to mourn, and a time to dance." Just to name a few.

Jeff, our youngest, is now our only. We have been tested many times but we always come away seeing God's hand in our destiny. Jeff will always be our baby. His hair is getting a little grey. He is handsome. He gives the best bear hugs. And you know he has given us the greatest gift of all–making us grandparents, and giving us a daughter-in-law to love. We were all together at a wedding recently. I loved watching him dance with his wife and daughters. He is a very good dancer. He takes after his dad. Dave and I also had a few good dances. Now is the time to dance.

It will take us from now to eternity to understand God's plan. Now we live by faith. Hebrews 11:1 tells us "Faith is the assurance of things hoped for, the conviction of things not seen." In other words, we need a firm belief that God is for us and not against us. I believe this.

I just have to say, "We love you, Lord."

DESERT MINISTRIES, INC.

Our purpose is to bring the living water of Jesus Christ to the various "deserts" of human life. We provide books and tapes and encouragement for clergy and laity. At present we have publications on *When You Lose Someone You Love, When a Child Dies, Christ Will See You Through, When Alzheimer's Strikes, A Journey Through Cancer, When Your Life Includes a Wheelchair,* and more.

We will gladly send a sample packet of some of our books and booklets without charge. If you would like additional copies of this book, please contact us, as follows:

Desert Ministries, Inc.
P. O. 747
Matthews, NC 28106

Website: www. Desmin.org
Telephone: 704-849-0109
Fax: 704-846-1530